IT'S ALL
ABOUT
THE
INCOME

IT'S ALL ABOUT THE INCOME

THE SIMPLE SYSTEM FOR A BIG RETIREMENT

MICHAEL LYNCH

LIONCREST
PUBLISHING

IT'S ALL ABOUT THE INCOME
The Simple System for a Big Retirement

ISBN   978-1-5445-3026-0   *Hardcover*

   978-1-5445-3027-7   *Paperback*

   978-1-5445-3028-4   *Ebook*

CONTENTS

Disclaimer.. vii

Foreword...xiii

Introduction.. 1

1. The Paradox of Retirement Income Planning.................. 11

2. Safety First!.. 19

3. Getting Risk Right.. 27

4. Two Out of Three Ain't Bad... 35

5. Win by Winning.. 41

6. How Long for the Rebound?..55

7. Building Blocks of Success 65

8. Assess Your Needs and Fix Your Target 79

9. The System Is the Solution...87

10. Let's Flex the Plan...95

11. Let's Add a Pension..107

12. Big Income Needs..115

Conclusion: Retirement Income
for the Modern World...127

Acknowledgments 135

Endnotes...141

DISCLAIMER

All opinions expressed in this book are solely my opinions and do not reflect the opinions of my respective parent companies or affiliates or the companies with which I am affiliated.

Investments or strategies mentioned in this book may not be suitable for you, and you should make your own independent decision about them. This material does not take into account your particular investment objectives, financial situation, or needs and is not intended as recommendations appropriate for you. You should strongly consider seeking advice from your own investment advisor.

*To my clients, each of you, who've let me share
your life's journey and taught me how to turn
assets into income amid the turbulence
that this world creates.*

FOREWORD

YOU'VE SPENT YOUR *ENTIRE* LIFE LIVING RIGHT, WORKING hard, saving through your employer plan, and perhaps even saving a bit in a Roth or taxable investment account. When you started, retirement was a distant goal, a vague concept. Now it's an approaching reality. Your gut tells you that you have enough money to retire, but your head is not quite sure.

You hear from some friends that you need $1 million and from others that $500,000 will get the job done. Prior to COVID-19, Bob at the office was incessantly fretting–bragging, really–that his $2 million stash wasn't enough.

One big question you ask yourself: *Do I have enough?*

This book will provide you with the tools and know-how to answer this question definitively.

But that's not why I wrote it.

Once you have enough, then what? Assets are fun to look at, play with, and brag about, but we live on income.

I wrote this book based on twenty years of practical experience helping hundreds of Americans turn their assets into sustainable *real* income. This is where the action is and where honest mistakes—both conceptual and practical—can cost you dearly. This book will teach you how to avoid these mistakes.

There are many bad choices you can make in turning your assets into income.

The first is spending too much and running out of money before you run out of breath. This terrifies many.

As with many tradeoffs in life, reducing one risk means exacerbating another. For your retirement planning, that's the risk entailed in not spending your money, not taking the vacations you want, and not purchasing the cars, toys, boats, or experiences you desire. Eventually, you will either get sick and die or, if you're lucky, simply die.

In the first instance, your diligence will feed the medical establishment, paying rent in the wrong kind of hotel.

You should have taken those vacations; the food and lodging were better.

In the second scenario of sudden death, your parsimony will enrich your children, nieces and nephews, or some charity.

Either you take vacations or your children will!

But even this is not the big mistake I see destroying retirements.

The big mistake is contracting "principal myopia," a common disease that infects Americans as they approach retirement. This disease causes investors and some advisors to focus exclusively on the risk of seeing the paper value of principal drop, if only for a month, quarter, or year. The reaction is to transfer to "safe" investments—anything with a fixed return: CDs, government bonds, bond-based mutual funds, fixed annuities. The result can be real financial pain, as you will soon see.

Relying on fixed assets in a world of increasing prices, if you're lucky enough to live a long life, is a path to certain misery.

I wrote this book to give you a systematic antidote to this terrible curse. Enjoy and profit from it.

Michael Lynch CFP®

INTRODUCTION

WHEN THE COVID-19 CRASH CAME HARD AND FAST IN March 2020, the financial press reacted on cue. "Coronavirus Shock Is Destroying Americans' Retirement Dreams," blared a representative late-March headline in *Bloomberg Businessweek*. The relentless narrative: devastated stock prices would dash diligently pursued dreams of retirement.

As I write in November of the same year, these articles have not aged well. They rarely do. As is often the case, the easy and the obvious will surely not be the real damage. Any person seriously planning retirement must prepare for these equity drops, which are temporary and fleeting.

The real damage is found in a far more volatile and destructive section of the financial market—one that more Americans have traditionally relied on for retirement security. A sector that has been under immense pressure for more than a decade.

This hit me like a baseball bat to the head in 2010 when Maria appeared in my office after listening to my *Smart Money* radio show. (And yes, I have been hit in the head by a baseball bat.) Maria's pained face told the story that something was not well in her world, and it didn't take her long to voice her distress. An immigrant, she'd spent her life working in Bridgeport (Connecticut) factories, never earning big money but systematically saving her way to relative prosperity. She was retired and had roughly $2,000 a month from Social Security and another $2,000 a month from her $500,000 nest egg that was safely secured at the local bank. That was before the financial crisis. By the time she got to me, the collapse of interest rates had slashed her interest income from $2,000 a month to roughly $2,000 a year. She was searching for solutions. What had she done wrong? How could she restore her income without risking her money?

FOLLOWING FORMULAS

Of course, Maria had done nothing wrong. She had diligently executed the sage American wisdom, forged in the crucible of the Great Depression, that nearly all my baby-boomer and Generation X clients can recite by rote.

The key to financial success:

- Get a good job and keep it.

- Spend less than you earn.

- Park the money in a safe place.

- Live off the interest, and never touch the principal.

Maria's problem—one she shared with millions of other Americans—was that this formula of success from the Great Depression collided head-on with consequences of the Great Recession. The result was misery for conservative investors—meaning millions of Americans.

A decade later, the plight of America's Marias had worsened. Interest rates rose intermittently, with the last surge coming in spring 2019, when people could again get five-year CDs paying more than 1 percent. Each time, however, political and economic forces slammed them back down.[1] In early 2020, after a year of increasing rates, the Federal Reserve cut the rate it controls to zero as a response to the COVID-19 catastrophe. If Maria's money was still in the bank, her income had dropped yet again, to at best a mere $2,750 a year.[2] Almost right back to where she was in 2009.

ADAPT OR DIE

Something is wrong. It's time for a new formula and a new definition of safety. When the world changes, we must change with it.

A series of paradoxes lies at the base of personal finance, none perhaps as perplexing as this: people live on income, not principal, but they fret endlessly about principal fluctuations. A closely related reality is that investments that allow principal to fluctuate tend to have stable income, while investments that protect principal value allow the income to wander like a leaf in the wind.

We all know that the stock market—that is, the value of the world's great companies—goes up and down. The press calls it "volatile" when it drops, be it 10 percent in a year or the occasional 30 percent in a month, as we experienced in March 2020. Yet over time, the ups are greater than the downs, as you'll learn as this book progresses, and years such as 2013 with a 30 percent positive return, 2017 with a 19 percent return, and 2019 with a 29 percent return are also volatile.[3] The point is that a 10 percent drop in stock price is proclaimed a tragedy by the press and therefore interpreted as such by many Americans. Yet it's always proven temporary and, interestingly for the juxtaposition I'm about to explore, not the direct result of any intentional government policy.

FOCUSING ON THE WRONG PROBLEM

What can be said of interest rates? Although we are trained to think of such things as CDs, bank accounts, government bonds, and even some corporate bonds as "safe," I suggest this may be a way of getting us to focus on the wrong feature. The principal value may be interesting to look at, but this focus obscures what's really important. That is, the economic return to American investors, especially retirees relying on them for income, is the interest these investments generate. This is anything but stable.

Consider the last thirty years, a reasonable horizon for a modern retirement. Ten-year Treasury rates, a good proxy for available returns on principal-protected investments, have ranged from 8 percent in 1991 to a dismal 1.72 percent at the time of this writing. The ride was jagged, with some ups bouncing off temporary lows, but the general trend is an inescapably painful 78 percent collapse!

The amazing thing about these unstable and perilously low rates is that unlike the random gyrations of the stock market, today's low rates—and the rates that ruined Maria's early retirement—are the direct result of government policy. Maria paid the tab for the Federal Reserve's expressed desire to reflate asset prices by keeping rates low. Ironically, this benefited borrowers, the very cause of the crisis, and sent the bill to savers such as Maria. She faced a reality of four options—none good:

1. Accept the 90 percent reduction in income by reducing her already modest lifestyle.

2. Spend the principal to maintain the life for which she had worked and saved for decades.

3. At this late date, invest her money in "riskier" assets in hopes that it will all work out.

4. Try to find a job in the recession to earn income once again.

Each of these options, to put it bluntly, sucked. There's just no sugarcoating it.

ARE LOW RATES THE NORM?

Neither I nor anyone else can accurately predict the future, economic or otherwise. Today's low rates may persist for decades. Alternatively, the chickens of years of reckless deficit spending may finally come home to roost, prompting a 1970s rerun of high inflation and high interest rates. Many happier scenarios may come to pass as well. I hope they do.

What I can do, and what this book will do, is to provide a modern system that is easy to understand and simple to implement and will enable you to generate the income you need in retirement, regardless of Federal Reserve policy and other events and circumstances over which you have no control. It's a system that should be embraced prior to retirement. Had Maria deployed this system even when she first met me in 2010, it would have resulted in both more income and more wealth in the following decade. It requires a new formula for success based on an updated understanding of risk and safety.

That was a bridge too far for Maria to cross, but we will chronicle it as if she did. If you're reading this book, chances are it won't be a bridge too far for you. Sit back and enjoy and benefit from her hypothetical journey. As you'll soon see, on the other side lies a robust system to generate high levels of retirement income and financial peace of mind.

1

THE PARADOX OF RETIREMENT INCOME PLANNING

A PARADOX LIES AT THE HEART OF MUCH RETIREMENT income planning. I often ask rooms full of pre-retirees a simple question: "Who among you has a primary financial goal to make your children rich?" Not only do few hands rise, but the room usually erupts in laughter.

The reality is that few people I encounter make leaving a financial legacy a goal. A common reply is, "We've already spent a lot of time and treasure getting them ready for life. This is our time. We want to spend our money. The kids can have what's left."

Not everyone has children, of course, and this same approach tends to apply to these individuals and couples. Few are amassing wealth in order to enrich a niece, nephew, brother, sister, or favorite charity or church.

This was certainly Maria's case. She saved her money to provide comfort in her retirement. Hence, the paradox: if your goal is not to make your children or anyone else rich with an inheritance, why are you so worried about what happens to the principal? If your goal is to enjoy your retirement, why don't you spend time worrying more about the durability and structure of income?

RECONSIDER WEALTH

This is a point worth pondering. We all live on income, not accumulated principal, but we define wealth as accumulated assets, not as inflation-adjusted monthly income. By traditional standards, Maria was just as wealthy when she arrived in my office with $500,000 in the bank generating a paltry $2,000 a year as she was a few years earlier when the same pile of cash was generating $2,000 a month.

That's standard accounting. Wealth is denominated in static asset value, not income flows over some period. But those standards miss something important. Maria was, in fact, drastically poorer than before, as her total annual income had collapsed by nearly half. Her investments were stable, but her income from her investments had dropped more than 90 percent.

What if it had worked the other way? What if Maria's income had remained at $2,000 a month, but her $500,000 of principal had dropped by 90 percent to $50,000? I suspect she might have been equally or even more distressed. Yet her material reality—her ability to pay bills, enjoy life, and stay in the world she'd worked so hard for so many years to create for herself—would have remained intact.

INCOME DRIVES YOUR LIFE

If you're still working, consider your current situation. One way I put market declines in perspective for working clients is by pointing out that if all their retirement investments dropped to zero but they kept their jobs, they'd be fine. If the opposite occurred—they lost their jobs but their assets doubled—most would be in a world of hurt. In other words, we are income dependent, not asset dependent. D'oh! For me, realizing this was a Homer Simpson moment.

For most of us, there is some level of inflation-adjusted income for which we would give up the right to ever own any productive financial assets if we absolutely trusted it would be assured for the rest of our and our spouses' lives.

That's right. You'd agree not to own anything!

GIVING IT ALL UP

This may sound crazy, but before you slam this book shut, consider an extreme example. You head a traditional family with two children, three grandchildren, and one more grandchild on the way. Yes, you say you don't want to leave them any money, that your retirement is your priority, but deep down you would like to send a little something, maybe an education fund or two, an occasional down payment for a house, and a little pile of cash.

Like Maria, you've been diligent, lived right, and sacrificed current consumption for future security, and you have amassed $1 million in various retirement plans and investments. If an entirely reliable source offered you and your spouse inflation-adjusted lifetime income of $250,000 a year after taxes, would you be excited?

Of course you would.

Would you still take the deal if you had to renounce ever owning another financial or valuable asset? That is, you'd have to not only give up your $1 million portfolio but also sell your house and cars and instead rent your home and lease your vehicles. We'd allow you to own your wardrobe and some jewelry, so long as none of it had much value. Would you take the deal?

THE GODFATHER OFFER

I'm not sure what your initial reaction would be, although I suspect there'd be some discomfort with parting with the house and $1 million. But once you reflected on the offer, you'd likely take it.

Here's why.

Under best thinking today, the $1 million will generate between $30,000 and $60,000 of annual income. Assume you live in a house that can be rented for $2,500 a month and your two cars can be leased for $1,000 for the pair. You'd be giving up at most $90,000 in annual value in exchange for $250,000 to replace it.

Remember the deal. You can't own any assets. There's plenty of ways to work around this fine print. You want to fund education for your grandkids. Gift a portion of your income to their parents for Section 529 plans or other education investments. You control the income, and you can turn it into intergenerational wealth.

Speaking of that, you might want your $1 million to double in retirement so that after a lifetime of living off the income, you could give each child a $1 million inheritance. This, too, could be accomplished with your income. Simply set up a trust and purchase a $1 million life insurance policy on yourself and your spouse, with the kids as beneficiaries. Again, you'll be using the "income" that pays the insurance premiums to generate assets for the future.

This example is unrealistic, impossible, and ridiculous. I get it. However, it does illuminate an often-obscured point: we live on our income, not our assets. So long as we have the former, the latter is really a sideshow.

The next chapter will examine what this means for safety.

2

SAFETY FIRST!

TAKE A GOOD LOOK AT THIS CHAPTER'S KICKOFF PICTURE. It represents a childish fantasy, an impossibility that may be conjured in happy minds but is never found in nature. In the financial world, this is a "safe" investment that produces high levels of reliable income. The key here is that safety is defined in the traditional, if anti-quated, way: as principal protected. You'll never lose!

In the last chapter, we explored the paradox that we all live on income, but we constantly fret about the condition of our investment principal. In this chapter, we will add this revelation:

- Investments and assets that keep principal stable and protected allow income to vary widely from day to day, month to month, year to year, and decade to decade. These include

CDs, US government bonds, and high-quality corporate bonds.

- Assets that allow principal to fluctuate produce more stable and balanced, increasing income. These assets include dividend-paying stocks and other equities.

UP IS DOWN AND DOWN IS UP

Ponder that. Investments that provide stability of principal result in fluctuating income. Assets that allow principal to fluctuate tend to produce more stable income.

Combine this with the last chapter's lesson that we live on income, not principal.

Now answer this question: Which is a safer asset for retirement—a well-diversified equity mutual fund or a US government bond fund or CD?

It's hard to accept and perhaps even harder to say, akin to New York Yankee fans realizing in 2004 that the curse of the Bambino was finally over for the Boston Red Sox. But I do think a redefinition of safety is in order.

SAFETY REDEFINED

Equity-based investments are far safer for retirement than fixed-income investments.

Recall the formula most of us have internalized for financial success—the very formula that destroyed Maria's retirement:

- Get a good job and keep it.

    * Check. Still a good idea.

- Spend less than you earn.

    * Check. Nothing is possible if you don't do this.

- Invest the money in a safe place.

    * Trouble ahead. We need an updated definition of safety.

- Live off the interest, and never touch the principal.

* Definitely throw on the scrap heap. Replacement: live on the returns and grow the principal.

The bottom line is that we need a new definition of safety for retirement income. The money you need in two weeks for the utility bill, in two months for your property taxes, and even in two years to purchase a motor home is only safe if the principal is protected. I agree. I won't argue with you and will encourage you to give up potential returns to keep your principal from loss when you need to make those payments.

But for your long-term retirement income that may need to last ten, twenty, or even thirty years, safety has nothing to do with principal protection and everything to do with inflation-adjusted income.

YOU CAN HANDLE THE TRUTH

Fasten your seat belt. I'm about to tell you something few others engaged in financial services will.

You don't need guaranteed principal. That's what purveyors of low-return banking and insurance products want you to believe. You don't need guaranteed income. That's what purveyors of depreciating products such as fixed-income annuities tout. You need inflation-adjusted income.

That's right. *Safety is contextual and means you need a dollar to be an actual dollar when you need to spend it.*

Most people will tell you that you need guaranteed income and principal.

Nonsense. You need inflation-adjusted or "real" income.

FIXED-INCOME DREAM TO NIGHTMARE

Did you ever consider what's so bad about living on a "fixed income"? That's never a term used with a smile. It's more likely used by a person to excuse not being able to do what they want, like go on a big vacation, dine out often, or even assist the next generation.

Flip back to the last chapter and you may be a bit puzzled. If your income were fixed at the level proposed in that chapter—$250,000, inflation-adjusted—there'd be no problem. But here on planet Earth, that's not the way it goes down—at least not here in America, where the Federal Reserve has a printing press and is committed to at least 2 percent inflation.

If your income is fixed and prices are not really fluctuating so much as increasing, your standard of living is being eroded. I like to fish, and I head out on the Housatonic River to Long Island Sound to get my dinner. The river and sound have currents. If I am not motoring at least at the speed of the current, I'm slowly drifting in the wrong direction.

That's the trap into which far too many retirees fall. They misunderstand safety and find themselves being carried into poverty by financial currents. Don't let that happen to you or your family.

What you need is a system that gives you what you need when you need it. That's the focus of the rest of this book.

3

GETTING RISK
RIGHT

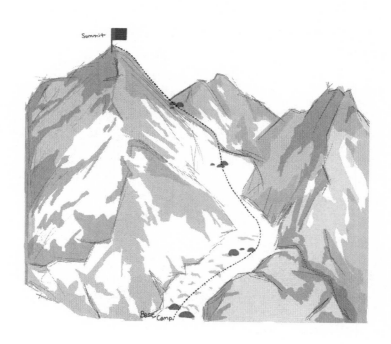

Examine the graphic above. This is Mount Everest. Imagine that you've been climbing mountains for years. You have trained hard and are ready for the big show. You're confronting this map of your next challenge. What's your goal?

When I pose this question in presentations, most people blurt out, "Get to the top." One or two get the answer correct: return to the base.

WHICH PHASE ARE YOU IN?

It's useful to divide your financial life into two periods: the accumulation phase and the distribution phase.

You climb the mountain during the accumulation phase. The disciplines that create success are dollar cost averaging, riding out the market declines, asset allocation, and rebalancing at both your lows and highs. You are not withdrawing money, so market swings are your ally, assisting you in buying more shares when prices are low and fewer when they are high. Stick it out, and history proves that this approach will get you the pile of money you need to retire.

Maria did fine on the climb. She probably could have done better with a diversified approach, but she nevertheless stacked up the money in what she considered a safe manner.

Descending the mountain is akin to your retirement, the distribution phase, in which care must be taken so you don't slip, lose your traction, and careen into a crevasse, never to be seen again. It's not that dramatic, of course. In retirement, you won't die suddenly, you will just be forced to move, cook at home during your staycations, and find new friends since you won't be able to keep up with your former crowd. After a lifetime of hard work and diligent savings, this will feel like a slow death.

The key to making it down safely is managing the risks of the descent. After all, gravity is working in your favor—until it isn't.

The risks include:

- Longevity: Living a long time, which is far more expensive than dying young.

- Market and timing: A kind way of indicating the annual 10 percent declines and all-too-frequent 30 percent declines in stock markets and the propensity for people to sell at the bottom.

- Inflation: The carbon monoxide of retirement—the slow, silent killer that turns a dollar into fifty cents.

- The unexpected: Disasters don't stop happening at retirement. Divorcing kids still need lawyers, and roofs need replacing. Other problems will keep arising.

WHEN A GOOD THING GOES BAD

Longevity is perhaps the most misunderstood risk. After all, living a long life is something most of us would prefer, especially if it's done in good health. How is this a risk? Living is expensive. Dying is cheap. Longevity means more years that need to be funded and more risk of inflation.

Poor financial markets are perhaps the easiest risk in retirement, if the scariest. History instructs on two points. First, financial markets will decline significantly at some time in most years and drastically every four years or so. It's easy to deal with because we can expect it, much like blizzards in New England. We know they will arrive. We just don't know the exact month, week, or day.

Market timing is even easier to understand but more difficult to address. If history proves anything, it's that the sun will rise in the east, gravity will pull us all down over time, and timing the market's sharp declines and ascents is impossible for humans and computers alike.

This does not stop a thriving industry from preying on the false promise that it's possible next time. It's not. The risk is twofold:

- Falling for the sirens, employing a market timing strategy, inevitably failing to get in and out at the right times, and slowly grinding down your assets.

- Neglecting to accept that the declines will come so that you don't have a plan to ride them out and you are forced to sell your investments at big discounts to pay your bills.

CARBON MONOXIDE POISONING

As stated above, inflation is the carbon monoxide of finance. It's a slow killer of both dreams and reality. Another way to put it is that termites do more damage than tornados. We worry about the tornados (i.e., the market drops). But they come and go, and we always recover. The real risk is the slow, steady, and relentless erosion from the termites. As with carbon monoxide, by the time you realize it's a problem, the damage is likely to be too extensive to remediate.

Bad things do not stop happening just because you're retired. You need to have a reserve for nonbudgeted expenses. Need I say more?

GET A PLAN

So what's the plan? You need three basic elements to address your retirement income risks. First, you need safety of principal. Now that I've spent more than a few pages dissing it, I'll tip my hat to it and admit that you need some US government-denominated asset that will never decline in nominal value. This gets you through the market declines and pays the unexpected bills.

The next thing you need is reliability of income. Chances are, you spent your working years earning one or more paychecks every month. You are accustomed to regular infusions of cash at predictable intervals. This helps you get through the downs of the markets and, to some degree, insures against living a long life because it's guaranteed for a lifetime. In addition, you don't need to ask

Maria about her pain to know that income that drops 90 percent cannot be considered reliable.

Finally, you need your total income to grow at least enough over time to keep up with inflation. No one says they are on a fixed income with a smile. You need enough of your money working for you to outrun the current and get your fishing boat up the river from the sound. That requires enough power to beat inflation. If you don't have enough of this, your retirement will succumb to the second law of thermodynamics and descend into irreparable decay.

NO SILVER BULLETS

Here's the rub. There's no single financial product or strategy that can address each of these needs. Assets that protect principal, such as US government bonds, bank products, high-quality corporate bonds, and deferred fixed annuities, don't grow the income and certainly don't provide reliable income over any reasonable long-term time horizon.

Financial products that provide reliable income, such as Social Security, corporate pensions, income annuities, and income riders on deferred annuities, don't provide for liquidity or safety of principal. Most don't offer much hope of keeping up with inflation. They do, however, ensure that you will receive nominal income for life.

Equity-based investments offer the potential for growth of both income and asset value. Over time the income has proved reliable, although it will decline in times of market stress. These assets cannot be relied on for safety of principal. In the short term, dividends and sales from gains will not prove reliable.

The bottom line: One type of investment will provide no more than two of the three benefits you need. You must create a system once you understand the benefits and drawbacks of each approach. More on that in the next chapter.

4

TWO OUT OF THREE AIN'T BAD

THIS CHAPTER IS INSPIRED BY THE LATE MEAT LOAF. Yes, it's capital *M* and capital *L*. Not the meatloaf you bake but the Meat Loaf to whom you've occasionally listened on your favorite classic rock station. "Paradise by the Dashboard Light" is surely your favorite, but I am partial to a different song, the riff of which is, "I want you. I need you. But there ain't no way I'm ever gonna love you." Kind of harsh. But then he follows it up softly: "Don't be sad. Two out of three ain't bad."

Thus it is with investment vehicles. Here's what you require of a properly functioning retirement portfolio:

1. Liquidity: A dollar needs to be available and valued at a dollar when you need to spend it. That is, it can't be reduced due to financial market fluctuations.

2. Reliable income: You've spent your life earning a regular paycheck, and retirement is no time to get accustomed to missed paydays and widely varying amounts.

3. Growth of income: Inflation must be met with at least equal force.

At this point, I don't think I'll get too many arguments on the application of this logic. After all, it's what we try to achieve quickly during our working years. Our priority is setting aside a cash reserve. It may earn a low return, but it's always available. We get a job and work to build a career that provides meaning but, equally important, stable and inflation-adjusted income.

Once retired, your investments must create that paycheck, unless you are to rely solely on Social Security or are fortunate enough to have a substantial employer-provided pension. Here's where our friend Meatloaf steps in. No investment vehicle meets all three needs.

Vehicles that protect principal and provide liquidity—mostly banking products and US government-backed bonds—don't provide long-term reliable income. That was Maria's problem. And they grow only if you don't take the income.

Vehicles that provide ironclad reliable income—pensions, Social Security, and individually owned annuities designed for income—don't provide liquidity outside the monthly payment. Social Security will keep up with inflation, or at least the urban wage index. Most other income-generating annuities have zero adjustment for inflation. In other words, the first check will be your largest in real terms, and inflation is the kryptonite to your pension's Clark Kent.

Vehicles that provide for growth of income—stock, equity, or ownership-based assets—tend to have the happy side effect of also growing principal. Often, it is this growth of principal that provides the income, as shares are sold to generate it. But the pure dividend streams, as we will see later, have historically generated inflation-surpassing growth. These vehicles are not stable in value and therefore do not meet our standard for liquidity. In addition, this income is the inverse of the fixed-income assets. It is relatively stable over long periods but cannot be relied on to maintain value over short periods.

The sad fact is that no single investment will love you completely. Investments aren't like dogs. But you can take solace in any investment likely providing two out of three things you need. The key to your retirement is understanding exactly what each of your investments will do, the need each will meet, and how to assemble them in proper proportions. Let's now turn to this understanding.

5

WIN BY WINNING

IT'S QUIZ TIME.

Over the last hundred years, what is the most frequent annual return of the broad US stock market?

- -20 percent or less

- -19.9 percent to -12 percent

- -11.9 percent to -8 percent

- -7.9 percent to 0 percent

- 0.1 percent to 8 percent

- 8.1 percent to 12 percent

- 12.1 percent to 20 percent

- 20.1 percent or more

Before you answer, please understand the question. I am asking for the modal average, or which range of returns represents the most common percentage accretion or loss from January 1 to December 31, with the cycle then starting anew.

I'm generally an optimist, and I know that America's largest publicly traded companies have a propensity to positive returns. Furthermore, I knew that the rough annual compounding of large US stocks is roughly 11 percent. I reasoned that the obvious answer wouldn't be the correct answer. So when I was presented this question by a representative of the Jackson National Insurance company, I guessed 12.1 percent to 20 percent. I figured I'd guessed right.

I hadn't.

When I ask clients to guess the answer, most pick a positive range. This is a good thing. Only one has ever nailed the answer: 20.1 percent or more. That's right: the most likely annual returns of the US stock market are not only positive but massively so.

Turn the page to gaze on an amazing visual.

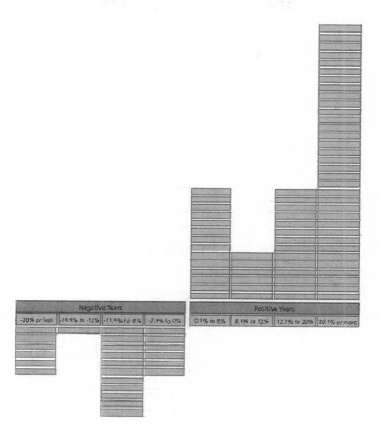

Source: Ibbotson SBBI Large Cap Index 1925-2020

SURPRISE!

This bar graph tells you what you need to know about the "volatility" of the US stock market. Of the 100 years, a total of seventy-five are positive and twenty-five are negative.

This means three years of increase for every year of decline.

Extreme declines of more than 20.3 percent occurred six times, not even once a decade. These are scary for sure.

Extreme advances of more than 20 percent occurred thirty-five times, or nearly six times as often. In other words, for every year in which an investor opened a December statement to discover a decline of 20 percent in value, they had six years in which every $100,000 in large-cap equity as an asset class jumped to at least $120,000.

Interestingly, the mean average of 8.1 percent to 12 percent occurred only six times as well. Markets both overshoot and undershoot the average. They simply overshoot more often.[4]

SORE LOSERS

We humans appear to be programmed to hate loss more than we love gain. Academics call this loss aversion, and it is well known to financial advisors and manufacturers of financial products. After the 2008–2009 financial crisis, the investment strategy of "win by not losing"

gained popularity. It's a seductive claim, based on irre-
futable, if basic, math. If a person can avoid the downs,
they will not require such large increases to achieve solid
average returns.

It also became popular to note the basic law of percent-
ages that requires a larger proportionate gain to get back
to the starting point after a loss. For example, a loss of 20
percent drives $100,000 down to $80,000. To get back
to even, a 20 percent bounce back doesn't do it. You'll
have only $96,000. You require a 25 percent turn to get
back to $100,000.

Peddlers of absolute return strategies, tactical allocation
portfolios, protected growth, and risk-managed portfolios emerged quickly from the wreckage of the 2008
financial collapse. Most came "back-tested" to show that
they would have protected people from loss in the recent
crisis. On the insurance side of the profession, products
offering principal protection with market upside flew
off the shelves. I often thought of this as akin to closing
the barn door upon finding all the cows had fled.

Each of these tools is useful in its proper place, and
I've used many with my clients. Still, one thing that
has been proven historically is that no person, institu-
tion, computer, or combination thereof can predict the
future.

Economic forecasts are unreliable. Market strategists are mere entertainers and soothsayers. Market timing is a losing game.

STAY IN IT TO WIN IT

People who worry too much about the downs are far more likely to lose by not winning than to win by not losing. Just look at the data.

I realize that the data presented above says everything about the past and nothing predictive about any particular year in the future. Financial history happened this way, but it didn't have to, and a few slips or changes here and there might have produced different results. If Winston Churchill had met his maker in South Africa or on the streets of New York, just two of his narrow escapes from death, who knows how the future might have been altered.

More recently, if the kitchen sink of strategies the US government threw at the debt-induced crisis of 2008–2009 hadn't worked, we might still be mired in financial misery. I can't argue with that. But so far, optimism is the only realism for long-run diversified investing in the United States. And what other options do we really have?

IF IT BLEEDS, IT LEADS

I focus on this because we are all bombarded with negative stories designed to keep our eyes on screens, scare us, and sell advertising. I'm not a psychologist, and I don't pretend to be. Yet, I can't help noticing that humans are far more attracted to negative than positive news across a broad spectrum of issues. "If it bleeds, it leads" is the adage of the local news business. Experts are always finding problems in a world that has been getting inexorably better across nearly every range of indicators. Meteorologists overpredict bad weather, not sunny days. This is called wet bias. Likewise, market commentators and financial writers focus relentlessly on what can go wrong rather than report what has already gone right.

Investing is an inherently optimistic activity. It's based on the belief that someway, somehow the future will be better than today, and you want to own the companies that are making it such. It's hard for pessimistic people to succeed, as there are always many good reasons to fear the future.

VOLATILITY IS A FEATURE, NOT A BUG

Consider the following graph. The solid bars represent the annual return of the S&P 500. That there are more ups than down is to be expected. What may surprise are the x's. Focus on them for a minute or two. These represent the largest drop that the index made in each year. Notice that even in years that are massively positive, there were often substantial declines, each scary in its own way, and many of which were no doubt heralded by experts as ushering in a "new normal" of decline and low returns.

KEEP YOUR FEET ON THE FLOOR

I think of these declines as misleading market signals to investors, similar to what head fakes are to basketball players. Most are false signals that, if heeded, will cause a poor result. In investing, heeding these signals results in getting out of the market at the wrong time and reentering at a potentially even worse time. The result is money not made, vacations not taken, and wasted worry. The basketball defender who consistently thrusts in the wrong direction will find himself driven around and scored on.

HOPE FOR THE BEST, PLAN FOR THE WORST

Now that I have evangelized the broad US stock market, I must provide a caveat. First, as I've said, just because

Win by Winning

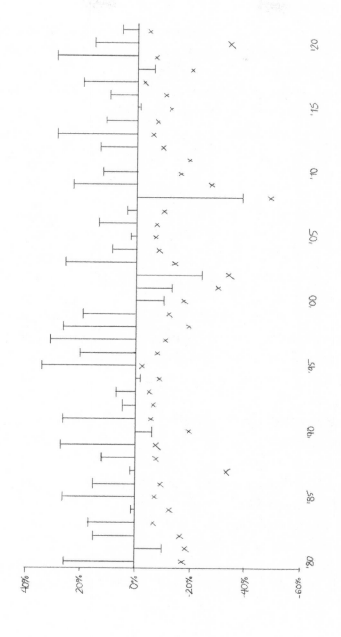

Source: S&P 500 1980-2020

51

history unfolded as it did doesn't mean it had to. Second, although the above data shows a pervasive positive bias in the broad US stock market, it would not be wise to simply dump your money in and let it ride without additional thought. The graphic below makes this clear.

There's a lot going on in this picture, so a guide is helpful.

First, the scale is logarithmic. The first tick represents 10 points, the next an additional 90, and the next an additional 900. This has the effect of muting the appearance of the increase.

Second, note the dashes at the bottom. These mark economic recessions. Something about modern economic policy is certainly working, as these painful periods are becoming less frequent and briefer.

Third, note that the climb is not smooth or predictable. History presents periods of both stagnation and sustained increase. Find your birth date on this graph and chart your personal course. I was born in 1969, so for the first decade of my life, investing would have been a frustrating experience. It would have paid huge dividends in the 1980s through 1990s, when the country reset its economic policies and the financial markets

Win by Winning

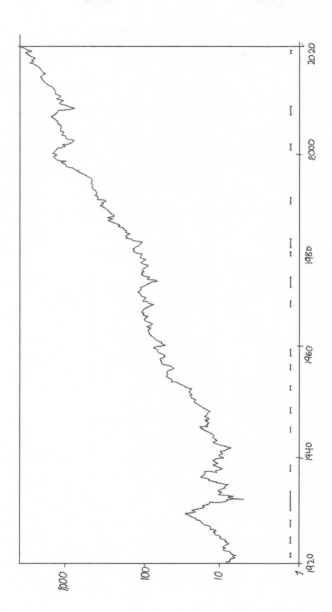

Source: S&P 500 1920-2020

53

performed well. In the 2000s, mid-career for me, we hit another sideways jag with two substantial declines.

Unfortunately, none of us gets to pick the exact timing of our life milestones—when we are born, start work, potentially support a growing family, retire, and ultimately die. As a result, we must employ a system that allows us to survive the down and flat times so that we can thrive in the good times. This system is the focus of the remainder of this book, after a brief detour to examine some stock market history.

6

HOW LONG FOR THE REBOUND?

THE CORONAVIRUS COLLAPSE OF 2020 SENT THE BROAD stock market first into correction and then into a growling bear at a pace few could remember and even fewer predicted. Markets hate uncertainty, and in the face of an unfolding government-mandated shutdown of large sectors of the private economy, investors struggled to price companies in many industries that were on hiatus. With little to go on, investors "catastrophized," working up a worst-case scenario and then believing that it was highly likely. First Trust Chief Economist Brian Wesbury noted that as of March 17, 2020, the stock market was predicting a collapse of 50–80 percent in corporate earnings. To put this in perspective, corporate earnings dropped 48 percent in the debt-induced financial crisis of 2008.

No one can predict the future—ever. We do know the reality of the present. For diversified investors in March

2020, that meant examining a portfolio that was significantly lower than just two months before. In reviewing the damage with clients, I more than once stared into pained eyes and was told that it took a decade for their investments to regain losses after the 2008 crisis and that, as a person in their sixties, they didn't have a decade this time.

I knew then this was wrong. It didn't take a decade after 2008. I also knew that the vast majority of people have an investing horizon far longer than one decade. But perception is often one's reality, and I set to work to put some facts to emotions. This is important when markets inevitably collapse.

YOU HAVE LONGER THAN YOU THINK

The first thing to note is that a person in their seventh or even eighth decade still has a substantial investing horizon. In my practice, I see few people slowing down in activity and spending in their seventies. Broad data shows average life expectancy of retirees is in the late eighties. Add to this the fact that our money is going to outlive most of us.

I still have an investment portfolio created by my great-grandpa, and he stopped being an active investor at least forty-five years ago when he died. Your real time horizon is unknown but likely decades. Finally, I note that you won't spend all your money at once. Rather, you'll withdraw it in 3–6 percent increments. This is why we create financial plans and have pockets of safety (e.g., bonds) in portfolios, substantial sums that are expected to increase in value at precisely the time when broad stock markets plummet. You must prepare to survive the bad times so you can thrive in the good times.

But what about the common belief that it took a decade to recover from the last bear market in 2008? In March 2020, I wanted to dig into the data to test this against real portfolio returns. One fantastic thing about financial markets in the information age is that all the price data is documented and can be retrieved. It's like statistics in baseball. We can disagree on judgment calls and subjective rankings, such as who the all-time best hitter is, but we all accept a game's pitch count, number of runs, hits, earned run averages, and batting averages. In investments, we have daily documented pricing confirmation that is stored for the ages.

IT RECOVERED QUICKER THAN YOU RECALL

To see how long it took to recover from losses after the 2008 collapse, I went to my Morningstar software and created both all-stock and balanced portfolios using real index funds with an added 1 percent advisory fee. I started with the 2008 crash, for which the prior peak of the market was October 2007. From top to bottom, the market dropped 57 percent.

Ten thousand dollars invested in October 2007 in an S&P index fund (of stocks) with a 1 percent advisory fee would have fallen to just under $6,000 at the end of 2008 and surpassed $10,000 again by December 2012. In other words, a five-year round trip, including five years from top through bottom to even and four years from bottom to even.

Running the same exercise for a balanced portfolio with 40 percent bonds and 60 percent stocks showed a quicker recovery. The $10,000 in October 2007 was fully intact by the end of 2010, a three-year journey from top to recovery and two years from the nadir to the starting point. Top to bottom back to top was three years, not ten.

Every crisis is different. The past does not predict the future, and although these are real investment opportunities, they do not represent any person's actual experience. Still, it's useful to look at a few others.

From March 2000 through October 2002, the broad US stock market dropped by 49 percent. It was driven first by the popping of the fashionable technology bubble and then by the horrible attacks of 9/11/2001, which we all can agree were a game changer in the economy and life in America and the world.

For the all-stock model, the round trip on this prolonged decline was roughly five years from top to recovery, with the value again surpassing $10,000 by the end of 2005. It was less than three years from bottom in October 2002 to recovery. The balanced portfolio surpassed the initial investment by the end of 2003.

For the last test, I went way back to the late 1960s, a time when I was growing in my momma's tummy. Like me, my index funds didn't exist then, but balanced funds did, so I modeled a fund that had been in existence since 1929. This period experienced two large dips: a 36 percent drawdown from November 1968 through May 1970 and a nearly 50 percent plunge from January 1973 through October 1974, during the so-called energy crisis and rapid inflation. For those who can remember, these were not good times.

So how did the balanced investment perform? An investment at the top in 1968 would have fully recovered by the end of 1971. An investment at the top in 1973 was whole again as we wrapped up our bicentennial celebrations at the end of 1976. At the end of February 2021, that $10,000 investment made in 1973 would be worth just under $1 million.

EVERYTHING'S GONNA BE ALL RIGHT

In 2019, I wrote that every crisis arrives with its own accent, unique triggering events, and underlying causes. Each must follow its own path from catastrophe to recovery. A novel virus and a vigorous government reaction to contain its health effects triggered the latest route. In March 2020, no one had any way of knowing the exact course the virus, the financial markets, and the real economy would follow. I said, "If we are to have a recession, let's hope it's limited in scope and pain. For those viciously attacked by this virus, let's clear the way for our doctors, nurses, and other healthcare professionals to vigorously treat and compassionately care for them. For our portfolios, which arrive in third place after the first two concerns, if history is a guide, they will be restored to health in a far shorter time than we may expect."

And that's exactly what happened in this instance. Thankfully, the recession was brief. Our healthcare system rallied, and the pharmaceutical industry produced effective vaccines in record time. Meanwhile, financial markets did what few expected. The S&P bottomed out at the end of March and was back to reaching highs four months later.

The COVID-19 experience is certainly unprecedented, but then, crises always are. Thankfully, we are working through it as we've always done. Remember these points and this experience when the next crisis arrives and your investments temporarily collapse.

7

BUILDING BLOCKS OF SUCCESS

People create great gains by concentrating focus. Put most of your eggs in one basket and then focus intensely on that basket is a formula used to build income, wealth, and to some degree, happiness. However, we preserve and protect wealth by diversifying and spreading risk. At that point, we spread out the eggs.

CONCENTRATED HAPPINESS

Consider the first point removed from the direct context of money. In love and happiness, we produce our big gains by concentrating our affection and attention on a single person. Of course, this has financial implications, but that's not the point here.

An example perhaps more directly related to finances is our "human capital." We concentrate our focus and risk by specializing in a trade or a single college major and then a career. Even in particular careers—such as law, medicine, and contracting—specialists tend to earn more than generalists.

One piece of advice I offer to anyone who asks is that the key to achievement is to be a meaningful specific rather than a wandering generality. I stole that from some-body—I can't remember who or I'd give credit.

SPREAD IT TO PROTECT IT

The opposite is true for generating retirement income. You've already specialized and used your human capital to amass a pile of financial capital. The task now is not to double it every five years and certainly not to take the risk of permanent loss that this would entail. You are tasked to deploy it in a manner most likely to produce your required inflation-adjusted income, no matter what the world throws at you. As Maria found out, something that appears safe may turn out quite risky under these terms. Returning to the last graphic in the previous chapter, you need a system to keep your money safe and the income flowing in the lean times as well as the fat years. This job requires a diversity of approaches.

THE SYSTEM IS THE SOLUTION

As I've explained, your system needs to provide safety of principal, an income reservoir for three to five years of income. This can be achieved only with low-interest, fixed-income assets backed preferably by the US government or perhaps a large insurance company. You are giving up growth on these assets in exchange for stability of and access to principal value. You are paying for it in potential gains forgone. Economists and other pointy-heads call this opportunity cost. Folk wisdom teaches nothing comes for free. As such, you don't want to overfund this bucket. Enough is enough.

GROW YOUR ASSETS AND INCOME

The next bucket—and, for most people, the preponderance of invested assets—is designed to produce growth of income. This will likely be a mix of stocks and bonds, but ideally it will be driven by equity or stocks. To see why this works, consider the table below, which illustrates the last thirty years of the S&P 500. It comes from the website Political Calculations. If you think this is too good to believe, I encourage you to spend some time playing with the calculator. Pick some particularly poor starting times, like the year of my birth, 1969, the crash of 1973, or even the peak before the dot-com bubble burst in 2000. This is recorded history, so have fun with it. You don't need to like it. You do need to believe it. It's what happened.

Look Back 25 Years to Look Forward: July 1996 to July 2021					
	Jul-96		Jul-21	Multiple	
S&P Value	$644		$4,364	6.8	Times
Dividends per Share	$14		$.58	4.3	Times
Earnings Per Share	$35		$157	4.5	Times
Consumer Price Index	157		273	1.7	Times

Source: S&P 500 July 1996 to July 2021

Over this period, you can see that inflation averaged 1.7 percent.

The principal value, dividends not reinvested, increased by nearly seven times. So the principal grew in real terms by four times, or 400 percent.

The income per share grew from $14 to $58, an increase of four times.

To review, the income outstripped inflation by four times; the principal outstripped inflation by two and a half times.

This is the engine that drives your real retirement income.

RELIABLE INCOME

The final element is reliable income. By this I mean a set amount that arrives at the same time every month and is in no way dependent on financial markets. This is another way of saying "annuities."

THE A-WORD

It's popular in some circles to hate annuities. A maverick money manager is spending millions to carpet-bomb American households with at least $500,000 to invest with this message via direct mail and social media. I agree with much of his entertaining critique but not all of it.

Furthermore, I know his target audience—middle-class Americans with the discipline to save and invest throughout their working years—does not hate annuities.

Social Security, after all, is a taxpayer-funded, inflation-adjusted income annuity. I don't know anyone who hates this income stream. I know most people love to receive it. Every election—regardless of who appears to be winning or losing—people fear that one candidate or the other will mess it up.

Let's dig into the structure of this much-maligned financial tool.

Modern annuities can seem complicated. I like to use a picture to explain the basic structure and terms.

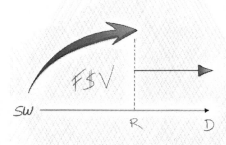

At the left of the drawing, SW stands for start work. R stands for retire, and D stands for die. It always seems to end the same way. Sorry.

The area under the curve represents the fact that an annuity, like any other investment, needs to be funded. This is called the deferred stage of an annuity. Common sense says that if the money is deposited, it must be invested in some financial assets. The F stands for fixed assets and fixed annuities. For these, the insurance company invests the funds and offers a set interest rate for a period, or an interest rate based off the performance of some other asset-class index. Money invested here is said to be in a deferred fixed annuity.

If the money is invested in financial accounts separate from the insurance company's general account, it is a variable annuity. Like other bundled investments—mutual funds or exchange traded funds, for example—these accounts will perform both positively and negatively in accordance with the fluctuation of the underlying securities, after all fees are deducted.

Speaking of fees, there are separate and fully disclosed fees for both the annuity contract itself and the individual investments offered within it. This annuity is called a deferred variable annuity. Like other securities, it is offered by a detailed prospectus that should always be read by anyone incorporating such a contract into their financial lives.

WHERE'S THE INCOME?

None of this has anything to do with income yet. Each of these examples is an accumulation phase vehicle. In this phase, the annuity looks, feels, and acts like any other investment with similar underlying assets. A fixed annuity, for example, acts like a bank CD. It comes with a stated interest rate for a set period. A variable annuity looks, feels, and acts more like a mutual fund account, with similar asset allocation.■

At the R on this drawing, we see the true purpose of these contracts for most people. At retirement, the horizontal line represents income until the D unfortunately appears. The line is flat. There is a reason for this: most private annuities do not adjust income for inflation. In this phase, the annuities are said to be in the income phase.

You can avoid the deferral phase completely if you like and simply use funds accumulated elsewhere to purchase a single premium annuity or income annuity. These are simple and easy to understand. They are also not very popular, as people recoil at parting with a large pile of money for a certain but far smaller income stream.

THREE WAYS TO GENERATE INCOME

This next piece of art is a graphic representation of the only three ways I know to generate income from assets.

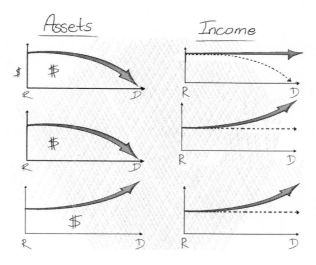

The graphic on the left represents a pile of financial assets, either real or imagined, yours or someone else's. The graphic on the right represents the structure of your income from this asset. Inevitably, both charts end with the D.

The first way to generate income is to take a fixed amount off a fixed-asset pile. If you know the exact date you will cease needing the money and the average and timing of the interest rates you will earn, you can self-liquidate your own pile. I've never seen this done.

In a bundled product, this represents a corporate pension or a fixed immediate annuity. Yes, many people still have employer-provided pensions.

The funds are liquidated over the recipient's lifetime; the income is fixed and keeps coming until death. That's the solid line. The dotted line below represents the risk to this approach. This line illustrates that inflation over time will surely erode the purchasing power or real value of this income stream.

TWO PROBLEMS: LIVING AND DYING

This approach carries with it two risks: dying too soon (thereby not getting much out) and living long through an inflationary period in which the real value declines. This is what happened to the pensioners of the sixties and seventies. Inflation is the pensioner's fiercest enemy.

THE THIRD RAIL OF POLITICS

The next pair of graphics represent Social Security. It's an inflation-adjusted immediate annuity. Here, you notice that the dotted line is level and the bold line slopes up. You will love this or already do. It's a lifetime of constant purchasing power. The only problem is that it's not enough to live on, so you need to supplement it. As in the first chart, the money pile driving this income stream, which in this case is the next generation's contributions to the system, ends with you and perhaps your spouse and will not pass to the next generation.

YOUR INVESTMENTS

The final pair of graphics is the money shot, so to speak. This illustrates the goal of most people's money management program. Notice that the area under the left curve is no longer declining. Done right, it's increasing. Most Americans do, in fact, end retirement with more money than when they started. This is not everyone's goal, of course, but it happens more often than one would expect. Your richest days may in fact be your last. Ponder that.

Perhaps more important, the right chart illustrates the role these assets will play in generating inflation-adjusted income. Done well, this part of your plan will double or more its share of your total income in retirement. The risk is that if done poorly—or disastrously wrong—the income will run out if the investments driving it drop to zero.

Prudent money management is the key to success. If all your eggs are in one basket—a dot-com stock, your fantastic employer's stock, urban real estate, and so forth—you may get fabulously rich, or you may be wiped out. If you seek too much safety of principal like Maria did, you can expect to face a retirement of diminished spending. A prudent balance of true diversification and sensible asset allocation must drive this critical bucket.

The next chapter puts it all together.

8

ASSESS YOUR NEEDS AND FIX YOUR TARGET

Up to this point, we've laid out the problem. Maria's focus on the old rules created financial misery in today's reality. Living on interest means living on nothing but Social Security. This is nobody's dream of a rewarding retirement. What your parents considered safe and secure promises only danger and disaster for you.

We examined what you need in retirement. Yes, you do need safety of principal, just not for all your investable assets. You also need reliable income, as your bills will continue to arrive reliably. Given ever-present inflation, you need your income to grow.

It would be nice if there were one investment or one financial product that provided these three benefits. That's the unicorn. It doesn't exist. It would also be nice if a Chevy Suburban delivered fifty miles to the gallon or if a Toyota Prius could tow a boat. These, too, are impossible.

Therefore, we explored the elements that you must use to create your retirement income:

1. Fixed assets for safety of principal.

2. Social Security, pensions, and private annuities for reliable income.

3. Stock or equity-based assets for growth of income.

The questions that you must ask and answer—which get to the art at the core of the science of retirement income planning—are how much of each element you need and how much of each you want.

FOCUS IN ON SPENDING

So far, I have not focused on retirement spending but rather on retirement income. There's a reason for this. I find lectures and treatises on expense management tiresome. Like the economist and the occasional CPA, they focus on the price of everything but the value of nothing. Studies show that, within limits, money can buy happiness.[5] And even if it can't buy permanent bliss, it can rent it for a while. As Chris Janson points out in his hit song, it can buy a boat and a truck to pull it.[6]

In my experience, most people who get to retirement having amassed a portfolio sizable enough to worry about such issues as asset allocation, income generation, and growth and protection of their money pile do not have spending problems. If they do, it's a problem of not spending enough. Chances are that if you make it to retirement with at least $500,000, you will take your last breath with just about as much money as you retired with.[7]

Spend. Take the vacation. Buy the Lexus, Lincoln, F-150, or maybe even Tesla if that puts a smile on your face. Be generous with your children and grandchildren. If you're tired of shoveling snow, head south or southwest for the winter months. It's your time. Use your money. If you don't, I assure you that your children or someone else will.

It's in the spirit of plenitude, not scarcity, that I admonish you to take the time to create a projected spending plan—a budget, if you will—for the early years of your retirement. This is key to the income system. Its purpose is not to hem you in, kill a retirement buzz, or remove the punch bowl from your retirement party. It's an acknowledgment of how the relative importance of income and expenses reverses on the day you leave your office, factory, or job site for good.

SPEND TILL YOUR END

While you work, your income tends to drive your financial life. It determines your income and payroll taxes, how much you can spend on life's necessities and even luxuries, and how much, generally, you can save. Once retired, it will likely be your expenses that drive how much income you need. (The exceptions to this are people who have large employer-provided pensions.)

A family that requires $10,000 spendable a month in retirement may have a very different system from a family that needs half that much to fund a fulfilled life. Even if their portfolios are the same size, they will likely structure their asset management and income generation plans differently.

This is not a hard exercise. Devote two hours to it, less time than it takes to book a weekend getaway, and you'll get it done. Gather your annual credit card summaries and bank statements. Online, you can sort the latter by debits. Download or contact our office for a spreadsheet with prefilled categories—or make your own from scratch—and fill in your expenses. This is what you spent last year. (If it's an unusual year—such as 2020 with COVID-19—pick another one.) Ponder your spending and ask what will change in retirement. For example, travel may go up. Recreation may go up. Dining out may go up or down. It's your life and your preferences, so don't ask other people what you should spend. Just estimate what you want to spend.

You've now generated the after-tax spending number that you need to live the life you desire. Unfortunately, this is not the end of the story. You have an indigent uncle to support. His name is Sam. The good news is that you will likely get to keep far more of your income in retirement than when working. But you still need to figure it out.

The first step is to understand how each of your income streams will be taxed both at the federal and your state level. This entire exercise can be accomplished quite efficiently by a tax professional or financial planner. But these instructions are guidelines on how to tackle it yourself.

BACK TO MARIA

I'll use Maria's case as an example. When she arrived in my office, her base spending needs were $3,000 a month. Prior to the debacle of 2008, she was spending closer to $3,500.

Maria's case was simple, as she basically had two asset classes: Social Security and a large traditional IRA. The rest of her money needed to come from her IRA. Since it is all taxed as income on the way out, a little understanding of the tax code helps us zero in on the pretax amount needed.

ROUGH IT IN

To figure out her pretax income needs, let's start with Social Security. Here, the taxation amount depends on your other income, so it is complicated, and software can be helpful. The maximum that will be taxed is 85 percent. However, if she could keep her taxable income plus half her Social Security under $25,000, she would not pay any taxes on her Social Security.

Given that she had $24,000 in Social Security, she needed $12,000 from her IRA to get to $3,000 a month. Add $12,000 from her IRA plus the $12,000 that was half her Social Security, and the sum is less than $25,000; thus, she would pay no tax on her Social Security.

We also know that she had a standard deduction of $12,400 plus $1,300 as a bonus for being over sixty-five. (Politicians love, respect, and fear seniors.)

Remember we are estimating here. Precision will come later. Once we subtract her standard deduction of $13,900, she would pay no federal income tax. Zero tax is my favorite rate.

Now let's add it up. She had $2,000 a month from her Social Security and $1,000 from her IRA. This generated

$3,000 in income, from which she would pay roughly zero in taxes. As you can see, at this level of income, the current tax code is very friendly.

Maria could now develop her asset management and income generation plan.

9

THE SYSTEM IS
THE SOLUTION

MARIA'S IS A SIMPLE CASE TO SOLVE. SHE REQUIRED roughly $3,000 a month of pretax income. Of this, $2,000 would arrive from Social Security. She needed only $1,000, or 2.4 percent, from her assets.

Stop and apply this point to your finances. One of the largest misconceptions I hear regarding financial independence derives from a failure to separate income needed from assets and total income. The result is a belief that retirement isn't possible or that it will come with a reduced standard of living.

It's easy to see why. Applying a 4 percent withdrawal rate, Maria would need $900,000 to support her lifestyle of

$3,000 a month. The number would drop to $300,000 if she appropriately restricted her need to equal income generated from assets.

GO YOUR OWN WAY

Don't be held hostage to someone else's income and asset needs. I hear it all the time: "So-and-so at work said I need $1 million to retire." The person is usually short of this, approaching retirement, and a bit despondent. I run their numbers, and often I am a bearer of good news: they are already financially independent or rapidly approaching such bliss. A leading cause of delayed retirement is the ill-informed workplace know-it-all at the watercooler, who may want coworkers to stay around and share the misery. Discuss sports or music but neither money nor politics while hydrating.

With her $500,000, Maria was financially independent, provided she implemented a prudent asset management and income generation plan.

Given that Maria had more than half of her income coming from the "reliable income" bucket, she had the luxury of focusing on the "safety of principal" bucket—her favorite and the source of her economic misery—and the "growth of asset and income" bucket.

Her annual income need was roughly $12,000 from assets. She should leave $100,000 in "safety of principal" assets and invest $400,000 in a diversified portfolio of equity-based and fixed-income assets. Since she was very conservative, a moderate portfolio of 60 percent equity and 40 percent bonds would likely be appropriate. However, I'd try to move her up to 70 percent equity because I feel that's better balanced considering her overall allocation.

SAFE ENOUGH

Here's why. One in five of her dollars—or 20 percent—were already in the stable value assets. If we add that to the 30 percent in bond or fixed-income assets, only one in two dollars would be exposed to stock market risk. Over the long run, this has been only the "risk" of increasing both asset value and income generated at a rate greater than inflation. You saw this in Chapter Two. But in the short term, financial markets can collapse suddenly without warning, and you must plan for this.

If you step back further, you will see that although half of Maria's assets would be subject to stock market risk, less than 33 percent of her income would be subject to this risk. More than half of her income was guaranteed and provided by the US government. I know it's not perfect, but at present, there is no better guarantor in the world. Focus narrowly, and she seems to be accepting risk. Pull back on your aperture, and her system's prudence and conservatism come into focus.

Counting Maria's income dollars, you'll see how this system works. She had $400,000 of investments generating $12,000 a year, allowing a roughly 3 percent withdrawal rate. Historically, she'd beat this with performance three out of four years (according to the Vanguard balanced index). She'd have more at the end of the year, after taking income, than she started with. In the one in four years of substantial portfolio declines, she could stop withdrawals on the portfolio and start drawing down her reservoir or safe account.

AN EVEN MORE CONSERVATIVE SOLUTION

Maria may balk at this solution. It's a large move from all cash to a preponderance of money that will fluctuate by the minute, day, week, month, and year without any predictable guarantees.

This is where annuities fit into a plan.

These are tools that provide both certainty in the present and guarantees for the future, subject to the claims-paying ability of the insurance company providing them.

We all have different tolerances for investment fluctuation and desires for portions of our income that we want guaranteed. During our entire lives, we accept risk with very few guarantees of our incomes, except the 1.5 percent of American workers who draw their checks from Uncle Sam. I'm appalled at the notion that new retirees suddenly need to be ensconced in some low-return, low-volatility plan for generating retirement income. It's as if we revert to toddlers who must be kept away from the world's many harms as well as its charms.

A BRIDGE TOO FAR

That said, Maria balked at my solution for a reason, and likely the $400,000 was a bridge too far for her to cross. In these cases, the insurance industry is more than happy to step in with many customizable solutions. In Maria's case, I'll examine just one.

Watching the pain on her face at the prospect of putting $400,000 of her hard-earned money directly into financial markets, I suggested she set aside $200,000 in a deferred variable annuity with an income rider. The deferred nature would allow her to retain control of the funds. This would provide some comfort. The income rider would allow her to withdraw a guaranteed percentage of these funds each year regardless of market performance. If the invested assets ever dropped to zero, the insurance company would provide monthly income for the rest of her life. This all came with restrictions and fees. Maria would need to understand it was a contract between her and a large insurance company. She would want to understand the nuances, definitions, and restrictions. She would need to read the prospectus. These tools are complex and not for everyone, but so are bulldozers, airplanes, and electric cars. Life in the modern world is often enhanced with the aid of complex tools.

In this case, she selected a contract that provided a 6 percent income stream while the money lasted and a guarantee of 4 percent thereafter if the funds ran out. This $200,000 now generated the $1,000 Maria needed each month. It increased her initial guaranteed income to 100 percent. It was not free, however, and the price Maria paid was not only the annuity fees but also the increased risk that inflation would erode the value of her income stream.

She now had $300,000 in complete reserve. In this system, she could keep $50,000 liquid for unexpected large expenses and invest $250,000 into at least a 70/30 mix of equity to fixed income. This would need to grow over time because it would be responsible for offsetting the effects of inflation on her annuity income. This plan secured all of Maria's initial income with guarantees.

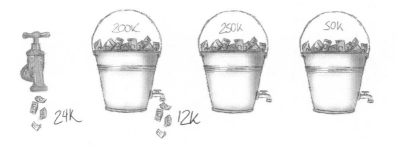

The future will always remain uncertain. No objective way exists to predict which of the multiple plans available to Maria would prove to be her best. There are scenarios in which her all-cash status quo would win—for instance, if interest rates spiked, inflation stayed low, and financial markets collapsed and this unlikely cocktail of misery persisted for many years. If financial markets perform as they historically have and Maria enjoys a long life, then the investment-heavy approach is optimal. Many scenarios exist in which the annuity approach wins as well.

There is no such thing as a perfect plan. However, there is the right plan for you and your family.

10

LET'S FLEX THE PLAN

MARIA'S CASE IS SIMPLE, INSTRUCTIVE, AND COMMON. Like our current tax code's standard deduction, it works well for nearly eight in ten Americans. It can scale both up and down depending on assets. It flexes to include such pleasant things as generous employer-provided pensions.

Keep in mind the task at hand—a lifetime of inflation-adjusted real income. Understand the job of each of its potential components:

- A government-backed pool to provide liquidity and principal protection when financial markets decline or even collapse.

- A prudently invested pool to provide increasing income from interest, dividends, and sales of appreciated stock shares.

- Annuity products from insurance companies
  that provide a contractually guaranteed
  lifetime income.

No part is perfect. As discussed in Chapter Seven, each provides benefit and carries risks. None always gives you exactly what you want. But blended properly, these ingredients will get you what you need.

Let's apply this to Bill and Sue, two big earners who were sixty-five and ready to retire. They enjoyed an upscale lifestyle and knew they needed $10,000 a month of spendable money to live their best lives. Bill looked forward to $3,000 a month in Social Security and Sue to $2,500. They had accumulated a retirement nest egg of $2.1 million in addition to a bank cash cushion of $100,000.

WHAT'S THE NEED?

Our first task was to determine the pretax income they would need to put $10,000 a month in their pockets. While working, it's not what you earn that counts but what you keep. When retired, it's not what you withdraw but what hits your account. If Uncle Sam spends it, you can't.

I used a spreadsheet model of the current year's tax code to project taxes. You can use your old tax returns, mock up a new one, or get help from a tax professional. This is an important step, especially for those with substantial income needs. Our tax code is extremely progressive at high incomes, and as you spend more, you pay disproportionately more income tax.

At present, Social Security is taxed less heavily by the feds than other ordinary and earned income. The maximum taxed is 85 percent of the benefit. So only $56,100 of Bill and Sue's $66,000 of Social Security would have to hit the federal tax brackets. After that, in this example we are assuming the $2.1 million of investments are in pretax employer plans. All additional withdrawals from these plans will be taxed as ordinary income. Based on the 2021 tax code, this couple would need to withdraw $70,000 a year, or roughly $5,800 a month, to meet their needs. This would produce pretax income of $136,000 per year ($66,000 + $70,000). The feds would get $13,200, or roughly 10 percent, and Bill and Sue would have just over $10,000 a month to enjoy retirement.

This set the target. Bill and Sue required $136,000 of pretax income to produce $10,000 a month to spend. Of this, $66,000, or just under half, was guaranteed by the US government.

TAX RELIEF

They planned to move to a state with no income tax, so for the first time in more years than they could remember, they would get to spend $9 for every $10 they earn. While working, they sent nearly 10 percent of their income to the Social Security and Medicare systems. Now it was time to take it back. To their surprise, taxes didn't appear to be a huge problem. That was a relief.

Back to the system. Bill and Sue had $2.1 million in assets to produce $70,000 a year in income. This was a withdrawal rate of 3.3 percent. At less than 4 percent, they were clearly in the safety zone.

They considered themselves to be middle-of-the-road or moderate investors and understood the need for capital growth to generate income growth. Still, they recalled the terror of the dot-com bust in the late nineties, the financial crisis of 2008, the brief but substantial drops in equity prices and account values in 2011 and 2014–2015, the Christmas collapse of 2018, and the COVID-19 dive in 2020. They wanted a substantial buffer to get through the bad times.

OPTION ONE

The first scenario they considered was all investments. They would rely solely on asset allocation to
buffer the downs. They would put a full five years
of required withdrawals, or $350,000, in low-yield-
ing but fully liquid government-backed fixed-income
investments.

This would leave $1.75 million to generate the annual
$70,000 target. They would invest these funds in a
well-managed portfolio expected to stay 70–80 percent
in equity-based investments. They would take monthly
withdrawals, use the sales to keep the portfolio in
balance, send the taxes directly to the government, and
spend what was left. Over time, the portfolio would be
expected to grow and the income from it as well.

The risks of this approach included having just over half
of required income subject to financial markets. Addressing this risk with the stable value bucket removed 16
percent of the investments from growth and income
production. These monies would not be subject to
market risk. They would not face inflation risk.

The advantages of this approach are simplicity, substantial reserves, maximum flexibility of use of assets, and expected growth of both income and assets in future years.

NERVES KICK IN

Something about this system made Bill nervous. More than half his income coming from unprotected investments didn't quite sit right with him. I advised Bill and Sue—as I do all clients—to use their head but trust their gut, and Bill's gut wanted a bit more certainty. So we moved to system two.

Here, we deployed an annuity strategy to supplement both Social Security and the pure investments. We researched many options, companies, and products. Sue didn't like the idea of the single-premium immediate annuity. Giving up a large sum to an insurance company merely to have most of the income return to her wasn't attractive. She worried about dying early but also living long, only to have inflation degrade the real value of the future income stream. She also wanted something left for her children and future grandchildren to inherit.

Bill felt that today's rock-bottom interest rates were an anomaly. He worried that large amounts of government spending and Federal Reserve money printing would eventually lead to inflation. He was old enough to recall the 1970s and remembered how being on a fixed income went from a great condition to one of a steadily diminished lifestyle. He didn't want to use any fixed or bond-based products for this reason.

OPTION TWO

Ultimately, they settled on the flexibility and transparency of a variable annuity contract that allowed them to invest in the financial markets through subaccounts but protect their income with a rider that guaranteed an initial withdrawal of 6 percent. This was 50 percent more than the safe rate from unprotected assets.

This sat well with Bill's gut. Sue used her head and knew that there had to be costs for these benefits. They studied the prospectus and noted both the fees they would incur from the invested money and the potential for reduced income in the future. All withdrawals would come first from their invested money. The guarantee would be activated if the account ran down to zero. At that point, the lifetime income would be cut in half to 3 percent.

NOTHING'S PERFECT

They understood the tradeoff. The product would provide more income early at the risk of less later. They would pay higher fees to guarantee that there would always be some later. Sue felt she'd spend more early in retirement, so she liked this feature. Bill, worried about inflation, understood that the guarantee might be eroded. Yet, he also knew that since he could invest the money in equity subaccounts, this product might grow in value and income. They both recalled an economics class they shared in retirement in which the professor echoed Milton Friedman: "There's no free lunch." Given the potential risks and rewards, they decided this was a lunch bill worth paying.

With this, Bill and Sue deposited $500,000 through direct rollover in a variable annuity with a guaranteed income rider. At 6 percent, this generated $30,000 of initial annual income. Add this to their Social Security payments, and they were up to $96,000 of guaranteed income, or 65 percent of their income need. Having two in three of his spendable dollars guaranteed put Bill at ease.

The income goal of $136,000 remained the same. Nothing in this change affected taxes. With $96,000 in initial guaranteed income, their remaining $1.6 million needed to generate only $40,000 annually. Sue noted that this move removed a lot of pressure from the invested assets. I agreed but quickly pointed out that it was properly understood as initial pressure—that is, pressure in the early years. Given the annuity's structure, they may need to make up more income from assets later because of inflation or a drop in the guaranteed income.

Bill and Sue decided that they needed less safety on the asset side since they needed only $40,000 a year in income from assets and had the preponderance of income guaranteed. They reduced the liquidity bucket from five years of income to four years and deposited $160,000 in this account. They invested the remaining $1,440,000 to generate $40,000 in annual income, or just under 3 percent per year. They derived comfort from knowing that the low initial withdrawal rate would likely allow for more flexible excess withdrawals in early retirement and provide the buffer needed in the later years if the annuity income were reduced.

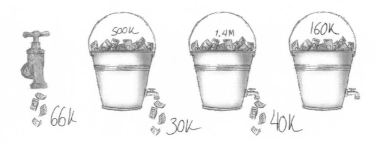

The system is a bit more complicated and a bit more expensive than the asset-only plan, but the couple reasoned that it's akin to always paying extra for safe, well-powered cars with all-wheel drive. They cost more to buy and run, but the comfort of knowing they had the power to get out of harm's way and the traction to make it through a blizzard was worth the extra cost. There may be no free lunch, but they liked what was on their retirement income menu.

11

LET'S ADD A PENSION

THE EMPLOYER-PROVIDED PENSION—MONTHLY INCOME from a company for which you no longer work—is a hoary part of the American past that never really existed for most of us. In 1970, at pensions' peak, just under one in two American workers worked for an employer with the traditional retirement plan.[8] Today, the number stands at one in five in the private sector.[9]

Let's meet two of them now, Tony and Toni. Tony was wrapping up a long career mousing around. He started at Walt Disney Company, hired right out of high school in the good old days when talent and on-the-job learning and performance meant more than a college degree. Toni worked first as a secretary and later as an administrative assistant for the local electric company. They grew up on the same street and married soon after high school. They were already grandparents and looking forward to retirement at age sixty-five. Toni wanted to start a free childcare center for her grandchildren. Tony planned to do whatever he wanted, which would likely include fishing in the Gulf of Mexico. They figured they needed roughly $9,000 in their pocket each month to live right.

TWO PLUS THREE EQUALS FIVE

Toni arrived at my office concerned that they were not ready for retirement. Because of the financial and other demands of raising and educating five children, she felt they were a little short in saving for retirement. When I asked Tony about the five children, he explained, "We had two boys, so we figured third time would be the charm for a daughter. Well, we were blessed with triplets, so we got two daughters and another son."

They were proud of getting five children through college without any student loans. "A college degree today is the equivalent of a high school diploma when Tony and I got started," Toni explained. "I wanted to get them ready to chase their dreams."

As a result, they had many years when there wasn't enough money for all of life's necessities and the important extras such as vacations, prom dresses, and retirement savings. Their combined retirement funds amounted to an impressive $400,000. Toni's friend Mary told her that a couple needed at least $1 million to retire, and Toni was worried she wasn't even halfway there.

At our initial meeting, I asked many questions, the sort one doesn't discuss with friends like Mary, and I was convinced they were ready to retire and move on to their next adventure. I discovered that not only did they have $54,000 in Social Security coming to them (Tony's benefit was $2,500 a month and Toni's $2,000), but they also had an equivalent sum in corporate pensions. At a 4 percent withdrawal rate, these pensions alone were equivalent to $1,350,000!

ASSETS PULLING LIGHT DUTY

The next time we met, I'd had a chance to crunch the numbers, and they looked good. With a target of $9,000 a month spendable, they needed just $10,000 a month in taxable income. They were in a sweet spot of the current tax code. Of the $10,000, their guaranteed income supplied $9,000, or 90 percent. They needed just $1,000 a month from their investments. This amounted to only 3 percent of their now impressive $400,000 pile. In retirement planning, size matters, but it's size relative to the need.

By now, you can probably design Tony and Toni's plan. Still, a little more background is needed to do it right. I discovered that they considered themselves conservative investors and didn't really like the downs but had always managed to sit tight and hang tough when the market got ugly. It was hardly surprising that they wanted to leave an inheritance for their children if possible.

They had plenty of income for today and could afford to go very conservative at this point. They were leaning in this direction, having again heard that it was important to go into bonds when retirement was imminent.

I explained that this may be riskier than investing more moderately. Today, they didn't need all their investments for income, given their fantastic pensions and solid Social Security. They faced the twin risks of a long life and inflation. Their pensions were not indexed for inflation. If inflation returned to just 3 percent, their pensions would be cut in half (in real value) when they reached eighty-nine. The job of their investments was twofold: they would top off their income need today and replace what inflation stole from their pensions in the future.

Given their conservatism, we placed $50,000 in an account containing fully liquid US government-backed investments. This provided five years of income insurance and left $350,000 to be invested in an

112

equity-dominated (70 percent) managed portfolio. From this, they would withdraw $1,000 monthly, with 10 percent going to the IRS and $900 free and clear to spend. Given that 90 percent of their starting income was already guaranteed, Tony and Toni did not need the benefits of an annuity. Their risk was inflation, and they benefited from the potential for growth of a pure investment solution.

If they'd been extremely conservative, they could have used a deferred annuity like Bill and Sue did. A deposit of $250,000 would have closed their income gap, and 100 percent of their needs would have been met with guaranteed income. That would have left $150,000 to replace the value of their income as inflation erodes it.

"That sounds like a belt and suspenders approach," noted Tony when I explained it.

"I was thinking an umbrella, raincoat, and hat approach," added Toni. We had a chuckle, and they explained they were fine with one layer of protection. "I guess we don't need $1 million," said a visibly relieved Toni. They had a simple, understandable plan and were ready to retire.

12

BIG INCOME NEEDS

EARLY IN MY CAREER, I LEARNED THAT THE FIRST difference between those who earn a high income when working and those who support an expensive lifestyle when retired is that income taxes take a larger cut of the top-line income during working years.

The second difference is that big earners—if they are commensurately big spenders—need to generate a larger portion of their income investments in retirement because Social Security benefits top out at $3,100 a month. As a result, they need to invest more in the accumulation phase, and they face more market and other risks to income in retirement. These are upper-class problems, but they are challenges that must be considered, addressed, and conquered.

HEADED FOR THE EXIT

These were exactly the issues with which Mike and Madison arrived in my office as the New England leaves were turning summer into a spectacular fall. Mike worked for thirty years as a highly paid outside salesperson for a technology firm. It was privately held and tightly controlled by the founding family. He followed the standard financial planning advice and maxed out his pretax plan. His employer topped it off each year to the maximum allowed by the IRS. It stood at $5 million when we met and was aggressively invested. Madison enjoyed her role as a homemaker and worked outside the home only sporadically, first as a classroom assistant in her son James's second grade class and later as an administrator at church when Jennifer, her youngest, hit high school.

After they finished funding their two children's college experiences, they suddenly had extra income. They invested in a so-called nonqualified investment account that added another $2 million. Mike was tired of work and ready to retire. They were adamant that they needed $25,000 a month in after-tax income.

Working off a $25,000 monthly spending need, I got busy. Based on the current tax code, I figured they needed roughly $375,000 of pretax income if they made good on their promise to move to a state with no income tax.

LACK OF RELIABILITY

Mike could count on $36,000 a year from Social Security. Madison was eligible for half of this, or $18,000 a year. Because her own benefit was less than this, the system topped off her check to half of his. Their guaranteed income, backed by the US government, was slated to be $54,000 a year, or just under 15 percent of their need. (Compare this with 50 percent guaranteed for Bill and Sue and 90 percent for Tony and Toni.) Their assets would be tasked with generating the other 85 percent.

I roughed out their capacity, and despite a sizable pile of money, they were $1 million shy of the amount I'd ideally want them to have. They needed their investments to generate $321,000 in annual income. At 4 percent withdrawn per year, they needed $8 million. With only $7 million available, they would need to set the initial withdrawal rate at 4.5 percent.

Mike was adamant that he was out the door. "If I stay on to make the million and I get there in two years with substantial saving and a little help from favorable financial markets," reasoned Mike, "the market could take a header, and I'd be two years older and right back where I am today. We've got what we've got. By any reasonable standard, it's a lot, and it's time to enjoy life."

As I listened to Mike, I recalled a recent study that demonstrated that, on average, a retiree's spending drops consistently throughout retirement.[10] Although I would have liked their money pile to be a bit larger, I knew we could make it work.

Madison recalled the stock market volatility chart I presented in an earlier meeting, which showed gains of at least 20 percent most frequently and downs in about one out of four years. "That chart makes me both hopeful and scared," she said, a bit puzzled. "I am hopeful because a 20 percent year will drive a seven-figure return, providing almost four years of income, and scared because a drop like 2008 to early 2009 will erase that much or more in a few days."

ADJUSTMENTS ARE POSSIBLE

At this point, we got philosophical and examined their budget. Yes, they wanted to spend $300,000 a year, but they didn't really need that much to be happy. The $40,000 budgeted for annual travel could be reduced in tough times. And they learned from COVID-19 that there were plenty of enjoyments right at home. Prices tended to drop in recessions, which meant dollars stretched further, and they would likely spend less in their eighties than in their sixties. They didn't want this factor built into their plan, but it provided a safety net—a buffer, a plan B—to which they could turn if needed.

We examined the three ways to generate income. Mike liked the simplicity of a 100 percent investment approach. He figured he'd been living his entire life without any significant financial guarantee by the government or anyone else for that matter. He didn't see a need to pay for that now.

As he voiced this opinion, I noticed that Madison's body language displayed discomfort, as she crossed her arms and locked her jaw. I asked for her thoughts. She was neither shy nor conflicted.

"I don't need $300,000 a year," she said, but she didn't want to rely on only the $54,000 from Social Security.

BUILD A BIGGER BASE

No one can predict the future, and she wasn't going to try. But just because financial markets have been favorable doesn't mean they will remain that way. She figured she wanted a base of $10,000 a month. Then she'd be comfortable with pure investments producing the next $15,000.

Mike found wisdom in her approach and knew from decades of marriage that it was wise to get on board with her insights. I set to work designing a plan according to these specifications.

The next time we met, I presented their asset management and income generation plan. They had $54,000 arriving each year, in monthly increments, from Social Security.

To get this to $120,000, I researched annuity solutions. Since Mike and Madison did not have a corporate pension like Tony and Toni did, they had to create a private solution. Given low interest rates, the pure annuity solution did not seem attractive. At their ages, they'd have to give an insurance company $1,365,000 to generate $66,000 a year for as long as each lived.

Alternatively, they could give a carrier $1,100,000 and generate the same income based on a rider guaranteeing a 6 percent initial withdrawal. It wasn't perfect. The fees were significant, and the income might drop later if the contract ran out of money. But this approach allowed them to retain some control over the funds and generate a high rate of income from them safely. They funded this with a direct rollover from Mike's employer plan.

This left $5.9 million to generate $255,000 of annual income.

The $2 million nonqualified investment account would be responsible for $90,000. Of this, $270,000 was placed in US government-backed stable investments. The rest was invested in a tax-efficient growth and income portfolio.

The remaining $3.9 million in Mike's retirement plan needed to generate the other $165,000. Of this, $500,000 was allocated to the stable account—inside an IRA to preserve tax deferral—to serve as a three-year income reservoir. Mike and Madison invested the remaining $3.4 million in an IRA allocated to 70 percent equity to generate the growth of both asset value and real income that they required to fund their best lives.

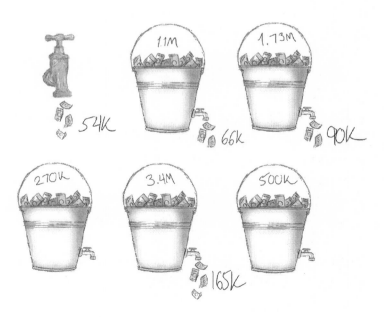

As we wrapped up, I projected a spreadsheet on my office screen that demonstrated their asset and income plan. Of their $375,000 in income, $120,000, or just under a third, was guaranteed. Two-thirds would be generated from unprotected but well-managed, fully flexible investments.

In terms of their assets, they had $770,000, or 11 percent, allocated to stable, US government-based assets to serve as an income reservoir to get through bad times and $1.1 million, or roughly 15 percent, allocated to a protected annuity that would generate 18 percent of the initial income.

The remaining $5,130,000, or roughly 75 percent of their money, was invested for growth and income.

"Who pays the taxes?" asked a now relaxed Madison.

"You do," I quipped, knowing that was not her real question. She frowned. "We will deduct them from your IRA withdrawals and send them directly to the IRS," I explained. "Social Security will do the same. Some years, you may need to make direct tax payments, depending on what happens in your nonqualified or taxable account."

They had one more important decision to make, I said, seeing they were ready to leave for a post-meeting meal.

What day of the month did they want their money deposited? Madison said she wanted the annuity on the first of the month. Mike picked the fifteenth for his IRA and the twenty-first for the nonqualified funds. Having set up near-weekly paychecks for retirement, they left for dinner smiling.

CONCLUSION

RETIREMENT INCOME FOR THE MODERN WORLD

WHEN THE WORLD CHANGES, SUCCESSFUL PEOPLE CHANGE with it. Our planet is littered with people and organizations that refused to accept that their "cheese" moved, to quote an insightful book, and ended up with skinny kids searching for a pair of Toughskin pants in front of a boarded-up Sears store.

For Maria, it was the old formula for financial success colliding with today's reality. Safety for your grandparents meant piling up stable currency, reinvesting the income until retirement, and then using the income to support a modest retirement lifestyle for a much shorter time than you can expect.

As Maria discovered, this formula leads to financial misery. It places your retirement income, the very thing you need to be stable, at the mercy of extremely volatile (and now extremely low) interest rates. At the very time in life when you don't want to have to change course, you are faced with a brutal choice: invest in what you consider riskier investments, consume your principal, or downshift to a diminished life.

When one door closes, another usually opens. This holds true of retirement income. Although interest rates have collapsed and formerly safe financial instruments have turned quite risky, there has been an explosion of effective financial products from which you can build a customized, robust system to support years of inflation-adjusted retirement income.

Banks and brokerages offer principal-protected, fully liquid assets. Asset managers and investment companies provide convenient access to low-cost bundled investments such as mutual funds and exchange traded funds. Insurance companies continue to innovate in their domain of expertise: contracts to generate nominal income protected for a lifetime. Independent financial planners stand ready to use these tools to build your retirement income house with brick, not straw or even wood.

The key, as Maria, Toni and Tony, Bill and Sue, and Mike and Madison illustrate, is using these tools to build a customized system, addressing each need with a tool designed to meet it, and managing the whole so you can adapt again when the world changes. These systems may not give you everything you want all the time. But they will get you what you need: a lifetime of real retirement income. With a little luck, you'll even have something to pass down to the next generation if you wish.

WE'RE HERE TO HELP

Congratulations on completing this brief book. If you've made it to this point, it's clear that you want to get your retirement income right. Now is the time for action and you have two options.

I wrote the book to provide you with all the tools to do it yourself for a robust retirement income system. Combine this focused book with my broader *Keep It Simple, Make It Big: Money Management for a Meaningful Life* (Lioncrest, 2020), and you have all the information you need to do the job right.

For some, this is an exciting challenge, and these will be but two pieces of detailed information they consume en route to managing their own retirement investment and income system. To you I say, go boldly. Enjoy the journey, and please reach out with any questions you may have along the way.

Experience teaches me that the do-it-yourself path is not the road many of you prefer to travel. For those of you in this group, life is short, and money management and income planning are not interesting, exciting, or fun. The process generates stress rather than joy. You know that life is short. You have today but maybe not tomorrow, and financial management is certainly not on your bucket list.

You want a trusted guide, a partner to design, explain, implement, monitor, and update your asset management and retirement income system. You want the income to flow and the money to grow, but you do not want to handle the money hoe. Tending the garden day to day, week to week, month to month, and year to year is a task for a hired hand.

I get it. I put all sorts of tasks in this category. If you are in this group, reach out to us via our website Simple-andbig.com or directly to mlynch@barnumfg.com. We will apply to be your hired hands. Our team of MBAs and Certified Financial Planning Professionals stand ready to answer your questions and help you design, implement, monitor, and adjust your plan. The first meeting is at our expense, not yours, and in our era of Zoom meeting, you don't even need to leave home to benefit from it. If we can meet all your needs in that meeting, we'll do so. If we can't help you, we'll tell you. And if we can add value, we'll make you an offer you won't want to refuse.

It's that simple. I look forward to making your acquaintance.

ACKNOWLEDGMENTS

ALL SIGNIFICANT THINGS IN LIFE ARE ACCOMPLISHED with the help of some people whom we know and many more whom we don't. A book is significant, so I'd like to thank those who I know helped make this one possible. Tasha Blount, Domenic Lynch, and Micaela Lynch top the list—Tasha by inspiring me with her temporary transition from artist to home flipper, all the while keeping our home a fun place for creativity; Domenic and Micaela by supplying much of the fun.

Sarah Butler had perhaps the single most important impact on this project. She illustrated the sketches under the watchful eye of her father and my junior high skater buddy, Jeff Butler. Jeff used to freehand punk rock T-shirts back in the day; my all-time favorite was a Replacements shirt I wore threadbare. I had Jeff in mind when I put out a call on Facebook for an artist. He replied, as I had hoped he would, but referred his thirteen-year-old daughter, claiming, "She's better than I ever was." Together, they were fantastic. Thank you both. Sarah, I hope the dough helps you get that horse!

Ethan Rauch filled a void I've long had in my life—a highly skilled and dedicated proofreader. After pointing out the many grammatical errors in my email missives, Ethan offered his proofreading services. Thank you, Ethan. You've made me look better than I deserve and made my mom's life easier, as I'd just received permission to run everything by her when you showed up. That said, thank you, Joyce Lynch, Mom, for your now secondary proofing role. Thank you for many other things as well.

Writing a book is one thing, but getting it produced while running a business adds complications. Sarah Rizk, Steve Cohen, Tom Melfi, Gorete Braga, Alisa Olsen, and Joe Riddell Jr. kept the business running and serving our clients. Thank you to our clients who provide daily inspiration and instruction. And thank you to all the support we rely on from Barnum Financial Group, starting with Paul and Mindee Blanco at the top; Allison Mislow, who keeps me teaching large groups; and Jyoti Naik and Lorraine Caggiano, who work with our compliance department to keep us coloring within the lines.

Those are the people I know. I'll conclude by thanking some I don't know personally but nevertheless appreciate. These are the reviewers at MML Investors Services, LLC, who, being charged with overseeing my financial planning practice, kindly review and approve all copy. That said, all errors are mine alone.

ENDNOTES

1   Libby Wells, "Historical CD Interest Rates: 1984 to 2021," Bankrate.
com, January 3, 2021, https://www.bankrate.com/banking/cds/histori-
cal-cd-interest-rates/.

2   This is based on April 10, 2021, best CD rates quoted on Bankrate.
com of 0.55 percent for one- and three-year rates.

3   JP Morgan Guide to Markets US 2Q 2021 As of March 31, 2021,
"Annual Return and Intra-year Declines," p. 17.

4   The above statistics are derived from "If You Think a Big Loss Is Painful, Try Missing Out on a Big Gain," published by Jackson Life Insurance company, January 2020. The index cited is Ibbotson SBBI US Large
Stock Index.

5   Honah Liles, "Money Can Buy Happiness: Here's How Much You Need
and How to Spend It, according to a Financial Therapist," The Insider,
October   24,   2020,   https://www.insider.com/can-money-buy-happi-
ness#:~:text=Money%20can%20buy%20happiness%20up,bigger%20
part%20of%20one's%20identity.

6   Chris Janson, "Buy Me a Boat."

7   Sudipto Banerjee, "Asset Decumulation or Asset Preservation: What
Guides Retirement Spending," Employee Benefit Research Institute,
April 3, 2018.

8   "A Timeline of the Evolution of Retirement in the United States," Workplace Flexibility 2010, Georgetown University Law Center, 2010, scholarship.law.georgetown.edu/legal/50.

9   Monique Morrissey, "Private-Sector Pension Coverage Fell by Half over Two Decades," Working Economic Blog, Economic Policy Institute, January 11, 2013, https://www.epi.org/blog/private-sector-pension-coverage-decline/.

10   Jonathan Guyton, CFP, "Why David Blanchett's Retirement Spending Research Is a Big Deal," *Journal of Financial Planning*, May 2016, https://www.financialplanningassociation.org/article/journal/MAY16-why-david-blanchetts-retirement-spending-research-big-deal.

Made in the USA
Columbia, SC
25 July 2022

63986073R00098